Table of

Introduction	2
Present Tense	14
Past Tense	27
Future Tense	39
Present Progressive	51
Past Progressive	63
Verb List	77

© 2018, Chris Hintsala. No part of this publication may be reproduced, stored in a retrieval system or transmitted in any form or by any means without the prior written permission of the author.

Introduction

I made this book for one reason. Over my years as an ESL teacher I watched my students struggle to build sentences. They would all do the same thing:

1. First, make a sentence in their native language.
2. Second, convert the words to English.
3. Third, try and fit the words into the complex grammar rules they had learned.
4. Finally, present a sentence with broken English.

After all of that work and all of those grammar lessons learned and they still couldn't make a proper sentence easily. This is because grammar is complex if you don't have the foundation to use it. All students can make basic sentences right away because they are simple. It is when they must add details and complex ideas that they all suffer. So to help my students, I created a way to build sentences without thinking about grammar.

Once my students started using this system, they couldn't believe how easy it was to make "big" sentences. For them it was a huge boost to their confidence. For me, it was a relief to finally have students making better sentences without grammatical issues. I realized that all along we had been teaching English to students academically. In a native setting, people never learn grammar first. They learn patterns as they start speaking. With this in mind I made my system. Instead of converting language to language and fitting it into a grammar rule, students should just build their sentences.

Now how do you build a sentence? Well I will show you.

Now I said you didn't need grammar and I really mean it but you do need to know 3 basic things before we can start. I bet you already know them.

The first is a **verb**. What is a verb? This is the action or activity that happens in a sentence.

The second thing is a **Pronoun/Name**. What is this? Well, it just answers the question "**Who**". They are: **He, She, It, You, We, They, I** or a **specific name**.

So what is the 3rd part you need to know? **Tense**. What is tense? Well it is just when the verb is occuring.

That's pretty much it. Of course there are many things we can add to a sentence but since this isn't a grammar book, let's call them **Details**. These details are what you will learn how to add in this book. These details make small sentences good and good sentences great.

Now that you know the 3 main parts of this system, let me show you how it works.

Example:

We need our 3 parts:
Verb: See
Pronoun: I
Tense: Present Tense

Now we need to **conjugate the verb**. How do you do this? I bet you already know this grammar from before but here is the pattern.

Pronoun/name + verb

Here our pronoun is **I** and our verb is **See**.

Conjugate the verb: I see.

*****Note: The only time this changes is for the pronouns: he, she, it and a specific name. Here we would add an "s", "es" or change the "y" to an "i" and add "es" to the verb.

Now let's add some details. **But how?** We answer simple questions with simple answers. The questions are ones that you already know, but I will explain them again. Here are the 7 questions and what they do:

Who: An easy detail to add when there is a second person in the sentence.
What: Usually this is an object (noun) or action (verb) in the sentence. This question happens many times in a sentence.
Where: This is the location of the action or event in the sentence.
When: This explains the time of the event or action.
Why: This is useful to help add a reason to your sentence. Commonly starts with "because, for, to" and then the reason.
How: This explains how an action or event occurs. Often starts with "with".
Which: This adds specific information to all detail questions above. Usually an adjective.

So now that we know the parts, let's put them together and build your first sentence.

First we need our verb, pronoun and tense.

Verb: See
Pronoun: I
Tense: Present Tense

Next we conjugate the verb to match the pronoun and tense.

Conjugate the verb: I see.

Now we can add our first detail. Let's look at this sentence and think which detail is the best one for the verb.

I see

    What? What do you see?
    Who? Who do you see?
    When? When do you see?
    Where? Where do you see?
    Why? Why do you see?
    Which? Which do you see?
    How? How do you see?

Hmm. We have many possible choices for the first question. But some questions are better than others. Think about it in your native language. Imagine someone is talking to you and they say:

I see….

Your first question to them is going to be?

What? What do you see?

And this is how you choose your first detail. Let's build this sentence.

Detail 1:   I see **"What?"** <u>a dog.</u>

Ok. Now let's ask another question.

I see a dog....
    What? What do you see the dog do?
    Who? Here who doesn't fit now.
    When? When do you see the dog?
    Where? Where do you see the dog?
    Why? Why do you see the dog?
    Which? Which dog do you see?
    How? How do you see the dog?

Again the first question you think of when your friend says "I see a dog..." is

Where???

This is your second detail. Let's build the sentence some more.

Detail 2:   I see a dog "**Where?**" <u>at the park.</u>

This is looking great. Let's keep building it.

Time for detail 3 so let's look at the questions.

I see a dog at the park....
    What? What do you see it do?
    Who? Who do you see the dog with?
    When? When do you see the dog?
    Where? Where do you see the dog at the park?
    Why? Why do you see the dog at the park?
    Which? Which dog do you see at the park?
    How? How do you see the dog at the park?

Which detail do you think fits best? There are many choices again. In this case I think **"What?"** fits best. Let's add it.

Detail 3: I see a dog at the park **"What?"** playing with a ball.

Now we have a really good sentence. I see a dog at the park playing with a ball. But we can do better than this. Let's add a 4th detail to this and really make it great.

I see a dog at the park playing with a ball....
  What? This doesn't fit easily now.
  Who? Who do you see the dog playing with at the park?
  When? When do you see the dog?
  Where? Where do you see the dog playing at the park?
  Why? Why do you see the dog at the park playing?
  Which? Which dog do you see playing at the park?
  How? How do you see the dog playing at the park?

The 4th detail can be more difficult on some sentences than others. Here we need to decide if it is good to add a detail or just make a new sentence. For this example we can add another detail. The best choice here is **"Which?"**. Which dog do you see?

I see a **"Which?"** <u>small brown</u> dog at the park playing with a ball.

Just like that you have built your first sentence. Most of my students can't believe how easy it is to think of writing sentences this way but once they switch their mind from writing grammar first to this style it gets much easier for them. Since each detail is so small, it is really difficult to ever make a grammar mistake.

Now that you know how to do this let's get started learning and building sentences for the 50 most commonly used verbs in the English language. By the end of this book and finishing every worksheet you will have successfully:
- Written 50 verb conjugations
- Written 50 simple verb sentences
- Written 50 good sentences
- Written 50 great sentences

That is over 200 sentences total!

So, let's get started building some sentences.

Present Tense

We will start in the **Present Tense**. This is the easiest time to get comfortable with the system. Present tense will allow you to focus on conjugating the verbs and getting used to the changes for the pronouns: He, She, It and a Specific Name. Remember:

Add an "s", "es" or change the "y" to an "i" and add "es" to the verb.

Now I will introduce you to the form that we will use for the rest of this workbook. Under the first few forms in each section of this workbook I will give you some helpful hints to keep you going but after the first few verbs, I am sure that you will be able to do this on your own ability.

Let's look at the form.

Verb: _____

Pronoun: _____

Tense: _____

Conjugate the verb: _____

Detail 1: _____

Detail 2: _____

Detail 3: _____

_____

Detail 4: _____

_____

This is everything we did in the Introduction but in a simple form to make it easy to build sentences. We will use this for every verb to make sure you see each piece of the sentence you build. I want you to answer each question simply. **Do not** try and add too much detail to each question. This will cause grammar mistakes. Just answer each detail question with a simple answer.

Present Tense

Verb 1 : <u>Ask</u>

Pronoun: <u>She</u>

Tense: <u>Present</u>

Conjugate the verb: <u>She asks.</u>

Detail 1: She asks_____Hint(Who)

Detail 2: She asks_____Hint(What)

Detail 3: She asks_____

_____Hint(Why)

Detail 4: She asks_____

_____

As an example, you could say: She asks (her teacher(Who)) (a question(What)) (about the test(Why))(tomorrow(When)).

Present Tense

Verb 2 : <u>Feel</u>

Pronoun: <u>He</u>

Tense: <u>Present</u>

Conjugate the verb: He_____

Detail 1: He _____Hint(How)

Detail 2: _____Hint(Why)

Detail 3: _____
_____

Detail 4: _____
_____

    As an example, you could say: He feels (happy(How)) (because he is playing baseball(What)) (_____(_____))(_____(_____)).

Present Tense

Verb 3 : <u>Hear</u>

Pronoun: <u>I</u>

Tense: <u>Present</u>

Conjugate the verb: I_____

Detail 1: _____Hint(What)

Detail 2: _____

Detail 3: _____

_____

Detail 4: _____

_____

As an example, you could say: I hear (_____(What)) (_____(Where)) (_____(_____))(_____(_____)).

Present Tense

Verb 4 : <u>Help</u>

Pronoun: <u>We</u>

Tense: <u>Present</u>

Conjugate the verb: _____

Detail 1: _____Hint(Who)

Detail 2: _____

Detail 3: _____
_____

Detail 4: _____
_____

As an example, you could say: We help (_____(Who)) (_____(_____)) (_____(_____))(_____(_____)).

Present Tense

Verb 5 : <u>Know</u>

Pronoun: <u>They</u>

Tense: <u>Present</u>

Conjugate the verb: _____

Detail 1: _____Hint(What)

Detail 2: _____

Detail 3: _____

_____

Detail 4: _____

_____

As an example, you could say: They know

(_____(What)) (_____(_____))

(_____(_____))(_____(_____)).

Present Tense

Verb 6 : <u>Like</u>

Pronoun: <u>You</u>

Tense: <u>Present</u>

Conjugate the verb: _____

Detail 1: _____Hint(What)

Detail 2: _____

Detail 3: _____
_____

Detail 4: _____
_____

As an example, you could say: You like (_____(What)) (_____(_____)) (_____(_____))(_____(_____)).

Present Tense

Verb 7 : <u>Bring</u>

Pronoun: <u>It</u>

Tense: <u>Present</u>

Conjugate the verb: _____

Detail 1: _____Hint(What)

Detail 2: _____

Detail 3: _____

_____

Detail 4: _____

_____

As an example, you could say: It brings

(_____(What)) (_____(_____))

(_____(_____))(_____(_____)).

Present Tense

Verb 8 : <u>Need</u>

Pronoun: <u>Michelle</u>

Tense: <u>Present</u>

Conjugate the verb: _____

Detail 1: _____ Hint(What)

Detail 2: _____

Detail 3: _____
_____

Detail 4: _____
_____

As an example, you could say: Michelle needs

(_____(What)) (_____(_____))

(_____(_____))(_____(_____)).

Present Tense

Verb 9 : <u>Think</u>

Pronoun: <u>She</u>

Tense: <u>Present</u>

Conjugate the verb: _____

Detail 1: _____Hint(What)

Detail 2: _____

Detail 3: _____
_____

Detail 4: _____
_____

As an example, you could say: She thinks

(_____(What)) (_____(_____))

(_____(_____))(_____(_____)).

Present Tense

Verb 10 : <u>Love</u>

Pronoun: <u>He</u>

Tense: <u>Present</u>

Conjugate the verb: _____

Detail 1: _____Hint(Who)

Detail 2: _____

Detail 3: _____
_____

Detail 4: _____
_____

As an example, you could say: He loves

(_____(Who)) (_____(_____))

(_____(_____))(_____(_____)).

Just like that you have finished the first 10 verbs out of the 50 we will study here. Now that you have learned how to build sentences you are ready to start a new tense. This doesn't change the pattern. It only changes the verb conjugation. You will still build sentences exactly the same way we have been doing it. Let's work on the Past Tense now.

Past Tense

Now we will start working with the **Past Tense**. When we conjugate the verbs they will have an **"ed"** unless they are an irregular verb. I have mixed in some irregular verbs to help you realize that the patterns for building sentences will not change. **Remember**: This is not a grammar book. This is a book that is teaching you how to build a sentence. This is the same natural way that children learn how to speak before they learn the reason (grammar) why they are speaking in that format. Learning the grammar patterns are best after you learn how to build sentences properly. We are training your mind how to think about building ideas so that you can make them in to great sentences. Also **Remember: Do not** try and add too much detail to each question. This will cause grammar mistakes. Just answer each detail question with a simple answer. **Super hint: All past tense sentences can have "When" as a detail!**

Now let's build some past tense sentences.

Past Tense

Verb 11 : <u>Hold</u>

Pronoun: <u>She</u>

Tense: <u>Past</u>

Conjugate the verb: <u>She held.</u> (Irregular)

Detail 1: She held_____Hint(What)

Detail 2: She held_____Hint(Where)

Detail 3: She held_____

_____Hint(Why)

Detail 4: She held_____

_____

As an example, you could say: She held (the ball(What)) (in her hand(Where)) (to throw it(Why))(to me(Where)).

Past Tense

Verb 12 : <u>Believe</u>

Pronoun: <u>He</u>

Tense: <u>Past</u>

Conjugate the verb: He_____

Detail 1: He believed_____Hint(Who)

Detail 2: He_____Hint(Which)

Detail 3: _____
_____

Detail 4: _____
_____

As an example, you could say: He believed (the woman(Who)) (from school(Which)) (about the letter he received(Why))(from the principal.(Where)).

Past Tense

Verb 13 : <u>Become</u>

Pronoun: <u>I</u>

Tense: <u>Past</u>

Conjugate the verb: I_____(Irregular)

Detail 1: I became_____Hint(What)

Detail 2: _____

Detail 3: _____

_____

Detail 4: _____

_____

As an example, you could say: I became (a doctor(What)) (_____(_____)) (_____(_____))(_____(_____)).

Past Tense

Verb 14 : <u>Give</u>

Pronoun: <u>We</u>

Tense: <u>Past</u>

Conjugate the verb: We_____(Irregular)

Detail 1: _____Hint(What)

Detail 2: _____

Detail 3: _____
_____

Detail 4: _____
_____

As an example, you could say: We gave (a present(What)) (_____(_____)) (_____(_____))(_____(_____)).

Past Tense

Verb 15 : <u>Make</u>

Pronoun: <u>They</u>

Tense: <u>Past</u>

Conjugate the verb: _____(Irregular)

Detail 1: _____Hint(What)

Detail 2: _____

Detail 3: _____
_____

Detail 4: _____
_____

    As an example, you could say: They made (a paper plane(What)) (_____(_____))
(_____(_____))(_____(_____)).

Past Tense

Verb 16 : <u>Eat</u>

Pronoun: <u>You</u>

Tense: <u>Past</u>

Conjugate the verb: _____ **(Irregular)**

Detail 1: _____ Hint(What)

Detail 2: _____

Detail 3: _____
_____

Detail 4: _____
_____

As an example, you could say: You ate (a sandwich(What)) (_____(_____)) (_____(_____))(_____(_____)).

33

Past Tense

Verb 17 : <u>Play</u>

Pronoun: <u>It</u>

Tense: <u>Past</u>

Conjugate the verb: _____

Detail 1: _____Hint(Where)

Detail 2: _____

Detail 3: _____
_____

Detail 4: _____
_____

As an example, you could say: It played (_____(Where)) (_____(_____)) (_____(_____))(_____(_____)).

Past Tense

Verb 18 : <u>Say</u>

Pronoun: <u>John</u>

Tense: <u>Past</u>

Conjugate the verb: _____(Irregular Verb)

Detail 1: _____Hint(What)

Detail 2: _____

Detail 3: _____
_____

Detail 4: _____
_____

As an example, you could say: John said
(_____(What)) (_____(_____))
(_____(____))(_____(_____)).

Past Tense

Verb 19 : <u>Tell</u>

Pronoun: <u>She</u>

Tense: <u>Past</u>

Conjugate the verb: _____ **(Irregular Verb)**

Detail 1: _____ Hint(What)

Detail 2: _____

Detail 3: _____
_____

Detail 4: _____
_____

As an example, you could say: She told (_____(What)) (_____(_____)) (_____(_____))(_____(_____)).

Past Tense

Verb 20 : <u>Turn</u>

Pronoun: <u>He</u>

Tense: <u>Past</u>

Conjugate the verb: _____

Detail 1: _____Hint(What)

Detail 2: _____

Detail 3: _____
_____

Detail 4: _____
_____

As an example, you could say: He turned (_____(What)) (_____(_____)) (_____(_____))(_____(_____)).

Way to go! You have finished the second set of 10 verbs out of the 50 we will study here. You have learned 20 new verbs and have made some amazing sentences. These are very detailed sentences. Showing you how easy it is to make big sentences like this will make creating and speaking normal sentences quick and easy. Let's keep going! Next we will work on the Future Tense.

Future Tense

Now we will start working with the **Future Tense**. When we conjugate the verbs they will have **"Will"** before the verb. The best part about the future tense is that the verb doesn't need to be changed. It is just the **"Pronoun/Name"**, **"Will"** to show future tense and then the **"Verb"**. That's it. There is nothing to change or remember about the verb for any pronoun.

Super hint: All future tense sentences can have "When" as a detail!

Now let's build some future tense sentences.

Future Tense

Verb 21 : Come

Pronoun: She

Tense: Future

Conjugate the verb: She will come.

Detail 1: She will come_____Hint(Where)

Detail 2: She will come_____Hint(Why)

Detail 3: She will come_____

_____Hint(How)

Detail 4: She will come_____

_____

As an example, you could say: She will come (home(Where)) (for lunch(Why)) (by bus(How))(this afternoon(When)).

Future Tense

Verb 22 : Be

Pronoun: He

Tense: Future

Conjugate the verb: He_____

Detail 1: He will be_____Hint(What)

Detail 2: He will be_____Hint(When)

Detail 3: He will be_____
_____Hint(How)

Detail 4: He will be_____
_____

As an example, you could say: He will be (a doctor(What)) (in the future(When)) (by studying medicine(How))(in medical school(Where)).

Future Tense

Verb 23 : <u>Find</u>

Pronoun: <u>I</u>

Tense: <u>Future</u>

Conjugate the verb: I_____

Detail 1: I will find_____Hint(What)

Detail 2: I will find_____Hint(Where)

Detail 3: _____

_____

Detail 4: _____

_____

As an example, you could say: I will find (my car keys(What)) (on my table(Where))

(_____(_____))(_____(_____)).

Future Tense

Verb 24 : Have

Pronoun: We

Tense: Future

Conjugate the verb: We_____

Detail 1: We will have_____Hint(What)

Detail 2: _____

Detail 3: _____

_____

Detail 4: _____

_____

    As an example, you could say: I will have (dinner(What)) (_____(_____))
(_____(_____))(_____(_____)).

Future Tense

Verb 25 : <u>Leave</u>

Pronoun: <u>They</u>

Tense: <u>Future</u>

Conjugate the verb: _____

Detail 1: _____Hint(Where)

Detail 2: _____

Detail 3: _____

_____

Detail 4: _____

_____

As an example, you could say: They will leave(the house(Where)) (_____(_____)) (_____(_____))(_____(_____)).

Future Tense

Verb 26 : <u>See</u>

Pronoun: <u>You</u>

Tense: <u>Future</u>

Conjugate the verb: _____

Detail 1: _____Hint(What)

Detail 2: _____

Detail 3: _____
_____

Detail 4: _____
_____

As an example, you could say: You will see (fish(What)) (_____(_____)) (_____(_____))(_____(_____)).

Future Tense

Verb 27 : <u>Want</u>

Pronoun: <u>It</u>

Tense: <u>Future</u>

Conjugate the verb: _____

Detail 1: _____ Hint(What)

Detail 2: _____

Detail 3: _____
_____

Detail 4: _____
_____

As an example, you could say: It will want

(_____(What)) (_____(_____))

(_____(_____))(_____(_____)).

Future Tense

Verb 28 : <u>Show</u>

Pronoun: <u>Omar</u>

Tense: <u>Future</u>

Conjugate the verb: _____

Detail 1: _____ Hint(What)

Detail 2: _____

Detail 3: _____
_____

Detail 4: _____
_____

As an example, you could say: Omar will show (_____(What)) (_____(_____)) (_____(_____))(_____(_____)).

Future Tense

Verb 29 : <u>Lose</u>

Pronoun: <u>She</u>

Tense: <u>Future</u>

Conjugate the verb: _____

Detail 1: _____Hint(What)

Detail 2: _____

Detail 3: _____
_____

Detail 4: _____
_____

As an example, you could say: She will lose

(_____(What)) (_____(_____))

(_____(_____))(_____(_____)).

Future Tense

Verb 30 : <u>Understand</u>

Pronoun: <u>He</u>

Tense: <u>Future</u>

Conjugate the verb: _____

Detail 1: _____Hint(What)

Detail 2: _____

Detail 3: _____
_____

Detail 4: _____
_____

As an example, you could say: He will understand (_____(What)) (_____(_____)) (_____(_____))(_____(_____)).

49

Way to go! You have finished the third set of 10 verbs out of the 50 we will study here. You have learned 30 new verbs and have made some amazing sentences. These are very detailed sentences and they are getting much easier now to make. You are starting to understand the pattern better and know what is the right question to ask next to build the details of the sentence. Now that we have finished the three most common tenses in the English language we will learn one of the two next most common. First up is Present Progressive. Let's build some sentences!

Present Progressive Tense

Now we will start working with the **Present Progressive Tense**. When we conjugate the verbs they will have "**~ing**" on the end of the verb. We also need to add a "**Be verb**" to each sentence.

Remember: He/She/It/Specific name: **is**

You/We/They: **are**

I: **am**

I know Present Progressive sounds difficult but it isn't. It just explains an action or activity that is happening right now. So imagine the sentence as you make it. What is happening at that moment in time? What action is playing out? Think about what is going on around the **Pronoun** when the event is happening. Use those details to help you build the sentence.

You are getting really good at building with the system now so let's build some present progressive tense sentences.

Present Progressive Tense

Verb 31 : <u>Begin</u>

Pronoun: <u>She</u>

Tense: <u>Present Progressive</u>

Conjugate the verb: <u>She is beginning.</u>

Detail 1: She is beginning_____Hint(What)

Detail 2: She is beginning_____Hint(Where)

Detail 3: She is beginning_____

_____Hint(Why)

Detail 4: She is beginning_____

_____

As an example, you could say: She is beginning (her homework(What)) (in her room(Where)) (for tomorrow's test (Why))(at school(Where)).

Present Progressive Tense

Verb 32 : <u>Get</u>

Pronoun: <u>He</u>

Tense: <u>Present Progressive</u>

Conjugate the verb: He_____

Detail 1: He is getting_____**Hint(What)**

Detail 2: He is getting_____**Hint(Why)**

Detail 3: He is getting_____

_____**Hint(Where)**

Detail 4: _____

_____

As an example, you could say: He is getting (an apple(What)) (to eat(Why)) (in the park(Where)) (while walking to play(How)).

Present Progressive Tense

Verb 33 : <u>Go</u>

Pronoun: <u>I</u>

Tense: <u>Present Progressive</u>

Conjugate the verb: I_____

Detail 1: I am going_____Hint(Where)

Detail 2: I am going_____Hint(Why)

Detail 3: _____

_____

Detail 4: _____

_____

As an example, you could say: I am going (to the lake(Where)) (to go fishing(Why))

(_____(_____)) (_____(_____)).

54

Present Progressive Tense

Verb 34 : Let

Pronoun: We

Tense: Present Progressive

Conjugate the verb: We_____

Detail 1: We are letting_____Hint(Who)

Detail 2: _____Hint(What)

Detail 3: _____

_____

Detail 4: _____

_____

    As an example, you could say: We are letting (Ari(Who)) (drive(What)) (_____(_____)) (_____(_____)).

Present Progressive Tense

Verb 35 : <u>Look</u>

Pronoun: <u>They</u>

Tense: <u>Present Progressive</u>

Conjugate the verb: They_____

Detail 1: They are looking_____Hint(Where)

Detail 2: _____

Detail 3: _____

_____

Detail 4: _____

_____

    As an example, you could say: They are looking (in the garage(Where)) (_____(_____)) (_____(_____)) (_____(_____)).

Present Progressive Tense

Verb 36 : <u>Move</u>

Pronoun: <u>You</u>

Tense: <u>Present Progressive</u>

Conjugate the verb: You_____

Detail 1: _____Hint(Where)

Detail 2: _____

Detail 3: _____
_____

Detail 4: _____
_____

As an example, you could say: You are moving

(_____(Where)) (_____(_____))

(_____(_____)) (_____(_____)).

Present Progressive Tense

Verb 37 : <u>Run</u>

Pronoun: <u>It</u>

Tense: <u>Present Progressive</u>

Conjugate the verb: It_____

Detail 1: _____Hint(Where)

Detail 2: _____

Detail 3: _____

_____

Detail 4: _____

_____

As an example, you could say: It is running

(_____(Where)) (_____(_____))

(_____(_____)) (_____(_____)).

Present Progressive Tense

Verb 38 : <u>Start</u>

Pronoun: <u>Micaela</u>

Tense: <u>Present Progressive</u>

Conjugate the verb: _____

Detail 1: _____Hint(What)

Detail 2: _____

Detail 3: _____

_____

Detail 4: _____

_____

As an example, you could say: Micaela is starting

(_____(What)) (_____(_____))

(_____(_____)) (_____(_____)).

Present Progressive Tense

Verb 39 : <u>Talk</u>

Pronoun: <u>She</u>

Tense: <u>Present Progressive</u>

Conjugate the verb: _____

Detail 1: _____Hint(Where)

Detail 2: _____

Detail 3: _____
_____

Detail 4: _____
_____

As an example, you could say: She is talking

(_____(Where)) (_____(_____))

(_____(_____)) (_____(_____)).

60

Present Progressive Tense

Verb 40 : <u>Write</u>

Pronoun: <u>He</u>

Tense: <u>Present Progressive</u>

Conjugate the verb: _____

Detail 1: _____Hint(What)

Detail 2: _____

Detail 3: _____
_____

Detail 4: _____
_____

As an example, you could say: He is writing

(_____(What)) (_____(_____))

(_____(_____)) (_____(_____)).

Awesome job! You have finished the fourth set of 10 verbs out of the 50 we will study here. You have now learned how to use 40 new verbs and have made some amazing sentences. To make the next section more challenging I will not be adding as many hints. You know how to build a sentence by asking the next question, so the last tense we will do is Past Progressive. Let's build some sentences!

Past Progressive Tense

Now we will start working with the last tense in this book which is **Past Progressive Tense**. The same as with Present Progressive, when we conjugate the verbs they will have "**~ing**" on the end of the verb. We also need to add a **"Be verb"** to each sentence but it will need to be in the past tense.

    Remember: He/She/It/Specific name: **was**
                            You/We/They: **were**
                            I: **was**

Since you can do Present Progressive easily, Past Progressive exactly the same but with a past tense **"Be verb"**. It just explains an action or activity that was happening in the past. So imagine the sentence as you make it. What was happening at that moment in time? What action was playing out? Think about what was going on around the **Pronoun** when the event was happening. Now let's build our last 10 sentences.

Past Progressive Tense

Verb 41 : <u>Call</u>

Pronoun: <u>She</u>

Tense: <u>Past Progressive</u>

Conjugate the verb: <u>She was calling.</u>

Detail 1: She was calling_____Hint(Who)

Detail 2: She was calling_____Hint(When)

Detail 3: She was calling_____

_____Hint(Why)

Detail 4: _____

_____

As an example, you could say: She was calling (her boyfriend (Who)) (after lunch (When)) (about going to a movie (Why))(later that night(When)).

Past Progressive Tense

Verb 42 : <u>Do</u>

Pronoun: <u>He</u>

Tense: <u>Past Progressive</u>

Conjugate the verb: He_____

Detail 1: He was doing_____Hint(What)

Detail 2: He was doing_____Hint(When)

Detail 3: He was doing_____

_____Hint(Where)

Detail 4: _____

_____

As an example, you could say: He was doing (his morning exercises (What)) (before breakfast (When)) (in his garage (Where))(_____ (_____)).

Past Progressive Tense

Verb 43 : <u>Keep</u>

Pronoun: <u>I</u>

Tense: <u>Past Progressive</u>

Conjugate the verb: I_____

Detail 1: I was keeping_____Hint(What)

Detail 2: I was keeping_____Hint(Where)

Detail 3: _____

_____

Detail 4: _____

_____

    As an example, you could say: I was keeping (my journal (What)) (under my bed (Where))

(_____ (_____))(_____ (_____)).

Past Progressive Tense

Verb 44 : <u>Live</u>

Pronoun: <u>We</u>

Tense: <u>Past Progressive</u>

Conjugate the verb: We_____

Detail 1: We were living_____Hint(Where)

Detail 2: _____

Detail 3: _____

_____

Detail 4: _____

_____

As an example, you could say: We were living (in a small apartment (Where)) (_____ (_____)) (_____ (_____))(_____ (_____)).

Past Progressive Tense

Verb 45 : <u>Sit</u>

Pronoun: <u>They</u>

Tense: <u>Past Progressive</u>

Conjugate the verb: They _____

Detail 1: They were sitting_____Hint(Where)

Detail 2: _____

Detail 3: _____
_____

Detail 4: _____
_____

    As an example, you could say: They were sitting (on a park bench (Where)) (_____ (_____)) (_____ (_____))(_____ (_____)).

Past Progressive Tense

Verb 46 : Put

Pronoun: You

Tense: Past Progressive

Conjugate the verb: You _____

Detail 1: _____ Hint(What)

Detail 2: _____

Detail 3: _____

_____

Detail 4: _____

_____

As an example, you could say: You were putting

(_____ (What)) (_____ (_____))

(_____ (_____))(_____ (_____)).

Past Progressive Tense

Verb 47 : <u>Use</u>

Pronoun: <u>It</u>

Tense: <u>Past Progressive</u>

Conjugate the verb: It _____

Detail 1: _____Hint(What)

Detail 2: _____

Detail 3: _____

_____

Detail 4: _____

_____

As an example, you could say: It was using

(_____ (What)) (_____ (_____))

(_____ (_____))(_____ (_____)).

Past Progressive Tense

Verb 48 : <u>Take</u>

Pronoun: <u>Karl</u>

Tense: <u>Past Progressive</u>

Conjugate the verb: Karl _____

Detail 1: _____Hint(What)

Detail 2: _____

Detail 3: _____
_____

Detail 4: _____
_____

As an example, you could say: Karl was taking

(_____ (What)) (_____ (_____))

(_____ (_____))(_____ (_____)).

Past Progressive Tense

Verb 49 : <u>Try</u>

Pronoun: <u>She</u>

Tense: <u>Past Progressive</u>

Conjugate the verb: She _____

Detail 1: _____Hint(What)

Detail 2: _____

Detail 3: _____
_____

Detail 4: _____
_____

As an example, you could say: She was trying

(_____ (What)) (_____ (_____))

(_____ (_____))(_____ (_____)).

Past Progressive Tense

Verb 50 : <u>Work</u>

Pronoun: <u>He</u>

Tense: <u>Past Progressive</u>

Conjugate the verb: He _____

Detail 1: _____Hint(Where)

Detail 2: _____

Detail 3: _____

_____

Detail 4: _____

_____

As an example, you could say: He was working

(_____ (Where)) (_____ (_____))

(_____ (_____))(_____ (_____)).

You did it. Congratulations!!

Now you have learned the 50 most common English verbs. Not only that, but you have made 250 sentences total (5 each verb) in the 5 most commonly used tenses. That is amazing. The best part of it all is that you have learned a different way to build a sentence. You have learned how to worry less about grammar and more about the 7 detail words because it is way easier to remember. Sure, in the future I encourage you to learn grammar so you can understand why you are making sentences this way or why those patterns exist. Learning that you don't need to learn complicated grammar to write or speak English is one of the best things I hope to teach you. It takes the most common complaint about learning a language out of the equation. How difficult grammar is.

Now that you have finished this book I encourage you all to watch the additional video lessons for more practice available on my YouTube channel. I have included a simple QR code so that you can easily have access to the playlist. I will also be publishing a follow-up book teaching you how to use what you learned here with building a sentence, to answer questions as well. It's awesome to think that what you learned from this book will also work for answering questions. And I will show you how in my forthcoming book.

Thank you so much for learning with me and I can't wait to keep teaching you more. It has been my honor to be your teacher on your journey to learning a new language.

Here is the direct link to the playlist for more lessons on how to build sentences. You can get additional lessons to help you study even more.

50 Most Common Verbs

Present	Past	Future	Present Progressive	Past Progressive
Ask	Hold	Come	Begin	Call
Feel	Believe	Be	Get	Do
Hear	Become	Find	Go	Keep
Help	Give	Have	Let	Live
Know	Make	Leave	Look	Sit
Like	Eat	See	Move	Put
Bring	Play	Want	Run	Use
Need	Say	Show	Start	Take
Think	Tell	Lose	Talk	Try
Love	Turn	Understand	Write	Work

Made in the USA
Middletown, DE
19 June 2019